Yellow Chested Swallow

Sherri Eisenhardt

BookLeaf Publishing

Presentation by *BookLeaf Publishing*

Web: www.bookleafpub.com

E-mail: info@bookleafpub.com

ISBN: 9789357617826

First edition 2022

For Aj, being the love I deserve without having to ask for it, supportive in the way I choose to pick up my own pieces, and fearlessly by my side.

ACKNOWLEDGEMENT

I'd like to thank everyone I've "lost" along the
way; without you, there'd be no inspiration.

PREFACE

Yellow Chested Swallow is the first in a pallette series. It tips its hat to the hermit and pays homeage to growth in isolation. This work was necessary to not only recognize how multi-tasking emotions are, but also to face loneliness standing strong, to zero in on what causes this within and give that to myself.

Present Tense

It seeps in sometimes
Like cold air into my lungs
I don't notice it's there
Until I feel
The crisp in my nose
Or the emptiness in my chest

Everything seems so hollow

I am one of the people
That call this grief beautiful
We are not wrong in this
But
This does hurt

The echo of
I told you so
When the first time
Should have been enough

How it's all so unbearable sometimes
Reaching in to nothing
And pulling back my own
Empty hand
Time and time again

Planted

Barefoot on the ground
Feet firm like
Shepard's roots
The loneliest tree
In the Desolate Yellow

Brain brawn fights bane
Heavy lifting
Yet remains in place
Slow in respiration

We do grow here
Not everything needs light
To thrive
Comfort in the isolation
The wind is not strong here
Nothing in the abandon
To make me sway

Graze in the depth
Until you become it

Engulfed
Encompassed
Enveloped

In fear of The Shallow

Autumn Leaves

When lonely extends it's hands
All the way from Kansas
To tell you
It found a new home
And her name is Mary

The montage of
A fake future
Flashes

And all the words
You wrote for her
And all the minutes
You spent waiting
Because she promised
It'd be worth it
Falls idle

Are you strong enough to be the bridge?
Even if she only needs you for a little while?

after A Happy Death

"It takes time to live
Like any work of art
Life needs to be thought about"

To affirm your solidarity
With the world
At its worst
To declare yourself life's accomplice
Even in its thanklessness
And its filth

How noble it must be
To walk hand in hand with
The very thing
That circulates despair
To show love and dedication
In the face of certainty
That it will not be reciprocated

To charge forward
With everything ugly
In the world
Riding coattails behind you
Feeding on each dredge
That kicks up dust

Without ego and pride
Because
The world is hopeless
But I love it anyway

To meet every face
Every emotion
With detachment and connection
Wearing acceptance and safety
On a bruised armor

It is your duty
To hold light to every corner
Of yourself
And show that you are
Both
The monster and the Saint
And you can't love properly
Unless you love
BOTH

Unabridged

In a world full of
"Look at me"
Surrounded by eyes in the dark

The dark
A place of content solitude
Full to the brim
Bursting at the seams

I am not alone
Because I feel alone
I am alone
Because
Of the peace I find here
The unapologetic choice
To exist on my own terms
In my own time
Completely free

Passive
Unbothered
Without need
Full and
Unabridged

Kiss Therapy

In the spirit of being bad lonely,
Or good lonely...
I suppose they're subjective

We try to kiss
Our way out
Or in
Depending on what side
You're on

And when we kiss
There are fireworks
Or maybe not

And after each
Pop
or light
or crackle
or flicker
or hiss
or screech
or boom

And after that
We see how fast

Our heart beats
Or doesn't
How fast we breathe
Or not

I was told once
That if you feel it
In your chest
It's fear

And if you feel it
In your stomach
It's instinct

But what if...
What if
I feel it in both?

What if...
After all the trial and error
After all the lessons and leaps
All the quality
And the freedom
And the love
The real love

What if we kiss?

Slow to Sentiment

Molasses movement
In adagio

The gnossienne of dark academics
The dusty corners untouched
The winding staircases into the deep
The stacks of words unread
The maps and journeys
Of stale roads

The light in my chest flickers
But the bulb refuses
To burn out

I am in constant requiem
For a place that does not exist
Paying condolences for tears left unshed

52 Hertz

The lonely emanates
Rippling outward
Butterfly flutters

The fatigue
The hot
The swollen throat
The blossom to serenity
The jasmine creeping slowly
Into the wild

Call after call
After call
After call

Heard but unanswered
The unbearable heavy
Of this repetitious symphony
Existing in the here and now
The calm bleak
Within the grim quake

Exulansis

There's a longing for comfort
When you're misunderstood
When your "peers" aren't actually
Your peers

See, when the things that bind you
Are not the same as the things that bond you,

When age and wage are your commonalities
And not your interest and intellect,
Not the things that make your heart race,
Not the way elegance glides from your fingertips
Like they're made to
Hide the imperfections of cracked pages

But the ones that
Teach you something
Show you meaning
Make you believe

And they do this
Ever so gently
Like turning the knob
On a safe

Guided by silence
Without force
Lacking pressure and threat

Rewards come in abundance

I'd like to think

I tire,
though

exhausted
in the disconnect

Cosmic Entanglement

It's all so violent,
To live and feel connected
The things we do
And say
And make
And break
In the name of love

How many times we've waited
For the dust to settle before
We stand up and brush the wreckage
Off our cheek
Only to fall again
and again
and again

How we wrap ourselves so deeply
Into each other
Only to recognize the vacant space
They used to hold
Long after the door closes
And the smoke clears

The unfolding feels like breaking
And you fear that healing will never come

You'll see thru everyone you meet
You'll go from nothing to a
new nothing
And each time
The same things rip you open

The spectators will all have different faces
But deep down are exactly the same
You'll ask them
Not to touch and
half of them will be deaf
The other half...
Leave handprints and maps to all
of the landmarks and mines

They don't see me.
At all.

Monachopsis

The change is constant
But I am still the only yellow
In a universe of blue

My lonely is a lingering scent
That jousts with laughter
The somber pitch in smiles
Unbalanced in disharmony
The dissonance of perfection

Trusting the unknown with your eyes closed

The In-Between

There will be times
When company feels
Like company
And the rooms fill with laughter

There will be times
When company feels
Like wind swept moments
That fall thru hands,
Slipping between fingers

Times where breathing is a chore
And it feels like waking up
Is an inconvenience

When dying is too much of a commitment
But sleep isn't enough
When the dread of interaction wisps over
And you just want to be carried away
To anywhere but where you are

Then you realize
You can dance with this or
You can fight it
You can move with it until

It feels like leaving

This is how you escape The In-Between

Ask the Dust

Walls can talk
And windows are eyes
Doors lock so others can open
There are chapters in life
Where we're told to
Not look in the rearview
And you'll know if
It just FEELS RIGHT

I want to ask the dust
I what to know what it knows
and see what it has seen
To hear what's been said to it
To know what it's like to FEEL
every feeling
But also to handle them
To be, long after they're gone
All the wiser

Dreary Embrace

Cold arms wrapped around me
Vacant breath on my neck
Collapsing,
Falling into myself

There's nothing left

The void is deep and blank
and I am left to think,
Intrusive and anxious,
Without direction in step

after The Day You Died
Because You Wanted To

"Who with a heart can stomach
how much we can stomach?"

The initial reaction is brave,
I don't care what people say
The wading
and sinking
and drowning
Are all acts of chivalry

The selfless art of real love
has painted masterpieces

Priceless

I will spend the
rest of my life
loving you and
you won't even be around for it

Origami Memory

Precise folds
Turn flat nothingness
Into works of art
Each crease creates
A new layer
An imperative part
A simple craft
As if to say
It's a means to become more
To make something from nothing

I scoff in jealousy

My life's work
no matter how I fold it
Is not a culmination of something beautiful
so much as sort of tragic

I cannot bend my arms
and turn them to wings
I cannot fold my heart to
make it smaller
I cannot makeshift
the elegance the trees have made

And when I unfold...
Breaking down in more
of a dance this time
Pirouettes are not mesmerizing
But defensive play

And when I unfold...
Love looks like
filling your cup
even if it means
emptying mine

And when I unfold...
Now I see the beauty
in falling apart

Cry Pretty

You're too pretty to cry
You're too pretty to cry
You're too pretty to cry
You're too pretty to cry
You're too pretty to cry
You're too pretty to cry

But not too pretty
to be lonely
to be lost
or forgotten
or seen thru
or passed over

Fain

Circumstantially happy
Acquiescence in tone
Unsure with one foot over the edge
Too good to be true
Inclination to RUN
Avoidant
Detached

But still reaching

Into The Outro

It starts here,
the beginning of the end
You see the finish line
just on the edge of sights

The illusion of depth
is objectively far
and vast

When you think too hard
eventually it starts to hurt
Laying here alone questioning your worth
Trying everything to make it work
But you don't know
who you are anymore
The person in the mirror
thinks waking up is a chore
That glow you had
is dimming now
Looking back at everything
you wonder how
How you got so far away from yourself
How you managed to fall
without a second thought
How many things they think and

do not say

Maybe it's better off this way

Maybe we leave and go
our separate ways
Maybe we look back and reminisce
about the good ole days
The mind plays tricks while the heart strays

How many things were said
without being true
How many times
did he lie when he said
I love you
Picking up the pieces
of my own heart
Glue them back together
and take a fresh start
Of everything I know
this is true
I'd burn every bridge if
it brought me home to you
To recognize the smile in the mirror
while I say

Maybe things are better off this way
Things are better off this way
Things are better

The Outro

They say that getting baptized
frees you from sin
brings you closer to God
You get to bear witness
and testify
of a new love you have received
You walk in light
have new character
receive forgiveness
accept salvation

Wash the world off of you

The problem is...

the world is what made you want this
convinced you this was real
moved you so

And now you're breaking surface
feeling no tension
and none the wiser

I would carry every regret
every selfish act

every human trait
and emotion
and want
and desire
and truth, no matter how ugly
without judgement.
Wear them with pride

Leaving with an outro
and maybe
a
little
less

lonely

.